This book belongs to ...

_____

GROLIER
BOOK CLUB EDITION

Maybe you should fly a jet!

Maybe you should be a vet!

By Theo. LeSieg
Illustrated by Michael J. Smollin

BEGINNER BOOKS A Division of Random House, Inc.

Text Copyright © 1980 by Dr. Seuss and A. S. Geisel.
Illustrations Copyright © 1980 by Michael J. Smollin.
All rights reserved under International and Pan-American Copyright Conventions. Published in the
United States by Random House, Inc., New York, and simultaneously in Canada by Random House of
Canada Limited, Toronto.

Library of Congress Cataloging in Publication Data:
Seuss, Dr. Maybe you should fly a jet! Maybe you should be a vet!
SUMMARY: Suggests in rhyme a variety of occupational choices. 1. Vocational guidance—Juvenile
literature. [1. Occupations] I. Smollin, Michael J. II. Title. HF5381.2.S48 331.7'02 80-5084
ISBN: 0-394-84448-3 (trade); 0-394-94448-8 (lib. bdg.)

Manufactured in the United States of America

Q R   1 2 3 4

Want to be a ticket taker?

Want to be a pizza maker?

Lobsterman

Jockey

TV fixer

Ballet dancer

Soda mixer

Do you want to be an astronaut?

Or keeper of the zoo?

You've got to do something.

What DO you want to do?

Tailor?

Sailor?

Nailer?

Jailer?

You've got to BE someone
sooner or later.

How about
a wrestler . . .

a writer . . .

or a waiter?

How about
a dentist?

How about
a florist?

How about

a forester working in a forest?

Do you wish to be an oil refiner?

Diamond miner?

Dress designer?

How about a paper hanger?

How about a bass drum banger?

Do you want to do your work outdoors?

Do you want to work inside?

Would you like to be a plumber ...

a policeman ...

or
a bride?

Would you rather work
in a mountain town . . .

or in the desert
lower down?

Pet shop owner

Money loaner

How about

a

slide tromboner?

How about a perfume smeller?

How about a fortune teller?

You could be a turkey farmer.

You could be a teacher.

You could be a lot of things.

How about a preacher?

You could be a clown!

Or a coffee perker!

How about
an iron worker?

Fireman

Tireman

Telephone wireman

Some girls make good picture framers.

Some girls make
good lion tamers.

Some guys make
good
tightrope walkers.

Other guys
are better talkers.

Maybe you should fly a jet.

Maybe you should be a vet.

How about a deep-sea diver?

How about a beehive hiver?

Would you like to be an actor?

Would you like to run a tractor?

Like to drive a taxicab? . . .

Or run a big computer lab?

Tennis pro . . .

Optometrist

Hockey pro . . .

Podiatrist

Chemist . . .

Lepidopterist

Glass blower

Mushroom grower

How about
a
fishbone boner

or a
roller coaster
owner?

Would you sooner
be a ballooner
or a grand-piano tuner?

Olympic champion?

Mountain guide?

It's not easy to decide.

You've got to be someone!
You can't just be a doodler.

You could be
a sculptor . . .

or, perhaps,
a noodle noodler.

You might be
a mystery guy!

Would you like
to be a spy?

Maybe you should be a vester . . .

a jester

or

a

hammock

tester.

Maybe you should be a voice.

Someday you must make a choice.
Maybe you should be a FOICE!
? ? ? ? ?

When you find out
what a FOICE is,
you can tell us
what your choice is.